What Do I Do When...

I'M WORRIED!

Danielle Haynes

PowerKiDS press.

PK Beginners

I'm worried. I don't know what's going to happen.

I'm learning to swim.
What if I can't do it?

I worry about many things. I think bad things might happen.

I worry I'll fall. Or get lost. I worry I can't do it right!

Worry can make my tummy hurt. Sometimes I cry.

When it's really bad,
my heart beats fast.

I talk to my mom and dad.

They say everyone worries. Even grown-ups worry.

It's important to tell a grown-up when I feel worried.

They can answer questions. They keep me safe.

Everyone feels worried sometimes. Now I know how to feel better!

Published in 2026 by The Rosen Publishing Group, Inc.
2544 Clinton Street, Buffalo, NY 14224

First Edition

Editor: Danielle Haynes
Book Design: Jeffrey Taylor

Photo Credits:

Photo Credits: Cover TimeImage Production/Shutterstock.com; pp. 3, 5 Sana Grebinets/Shutterstock.com; p. 7 Hananeko_Studio/Shutterstock.com; p. 9 Ermolaev Alexander/Shutterstock.com; p. 11 220 Selfmade studio/Shutterstock.com; p. 13 Luis Molinero/Shutterstock.com; p. 15 La Famiglia/Shutterstock.com; p. 17 Zivica Kerkez/Shutterstock.com; pp. 19, 21 nimito/Shutterstock.com; p. 23 Ermolaev Alexander/Shutterstock.com.

Cataloging-in-Publication Data
Names: Haynes, Danielle.
Title: I'm worried! / Danielle Haynes.
Description: Buffalo, New York : PowerKids Press, 2026. | Series: What do I do when...
Identifiers: ISBN 9781499456042 (pbk.) | ISBN 9781499456059 (library bound) | ISBN 9781499456066 (ebook)
Subjects: LCSH: Worry in children--Juvenile literature. | Worry--Juvenile literature. | Emotions in children--Juvenile literature.
Classification: LCC BF723.W67 H39 2026 | DDC 155.41246--dc23

Manufactured in China

CPSIA Compliance Information: Batch #QWPK26. For further information contact Rosen Publishing at 1-800-237-9932.